Hitler and the Germans

Ronald Gray

Published in cooperation with Cambridge University Press
Lerner Publications Company, Minneapolis

LIBRARY OF CONGRESS CATALOGING IN PUBLICATION DATA

Gray, Ronald D.
    Hitler and the Germans.

    (A Cambridge topic book)
    Includes index.
    Summary: Examines how and why Hitler and the Nazis
came to power, raising the question of whether such a
thing could happen again.
    1. Germany—History—1933-1945—Juvenile literature.
2. Germany—History—20th century—Juvenile literature.
3. Hitler, Adolf, 1889-1945—Juvenile literature.
[1. Germany—History—20th century. 2. Hitler, Adolf,
1889-1945] I. Title. II. Series.
DD256.5.G715 1983   943.086′092′4   83-996
ISBN 0-8225-1231-9 (lib. bdg.)

This edition first published 1983 by Lerner Publications Company
by permission of Cambridge University Press.

Original edition copyright © 1981 by Cambridge University Press
as part of *The Cambridge Introduction to the History of Mankind: Topic Book.*

International Standard Book Number: 0-8225-1231-9
Library of Congress Catalog Card Number: 83-996

Manufactured in the United States of America

This edition is available exclusively from:
Lerner Publications Company, 241 First Avenue North, Minneapolis, Minnesota 55401

1 2 3 4 5 6 7 8 9 10 92 91 90 89 88 87 86 85 84 83

Contents

1 **The fall of imperial Germany** *p.4*
The Second Reich *p.4*
The Great War *p.4*
Revolution *p.5*
Humiliation *p.6*

2 **The rise of the Weimar Republic** *p.7*
The years of poverty and shame *p.7*
New nationalism *p.8*
Hitler's early years *p.8*
Weimar succeeds *p.9*

3 **Economic crisis and Nazi takeover** *p.11*
The Wall Street crash *p.11*
How the Nazis gained support *p.12*
Events of 1932 *p.13*
Gaining complete control *p.13*

4 **The Third Reich** *p.15*
The Nazi State *p.15*
The racial creed *p.16*
The rule of the SS *p.17*

Why did the Germans support Hitler? *p.18*
Hitler brings back prosperity *p.19*
Hitler brings back respect *p.20*
The leaders of the Third Reich *p.22*

5 **The new order in Europe** *p.24*
Conquest without peace *p.24*
The struggle against Communism *p.25*
Europe under the terror *p.26*
Why did the Germans support the war? *p.28*
The destruction of Germany *p.29*

6 **Hitler's legacy** *p.30*
Human rights and human duty *p.30*
Germany divided *p.31*
The legend *p.31*

The Hitler years. Key dates *p.32*

Index p. 33
Acknowledgments p. 35

Introduction

At the beginning of this century the Germans were, by all normal standards, one of the most civilised nations in the world. Under Hitler they came to use their skill and strength to support and spread a tyranny which mocked at civilised values. The Nazis, Hitler's followers, despised freedom, tolerance, reasoned argument and ordinary human decency; they used lies, mob hysteria and terror; they inflicted torture, slavery and massacre on millions of innocent people. If Hitler had won, civilisation in Europe could well have come to an end. Even though he died in defeat the cruelties that the Germans inflicted between 1933 and 1945 under Nazi rule have all too often been copied by others.

How could such things have come about? How could such a man as Hitler, apparently insignificant and absurd, rise within a few years to absolute and terrible power? Was it because of a freak combination of conditions, an accident not likely to happen again? Or could something similar easily befall other civilised peoples?

The questions have been asked often and anxiously, and there is no certain answer. This book attempts to state the story simply and to offer some possible explanations.

1 The fall of imperial Germany

The Second Reich

In the last quarter of the nineteenth century, Germany changed completely. It had once been a land divided into kingdoms, duchies, counties and free cities, with few factories and railways. The Industrial Revolution in Germany began late, about 1840. Yet by 1910 Germany's annual share in world-trade was greater than that of the USA, second only to Britain's. The population had grown rapidly, from 41 millions in 1871 to 65 millions in 1911. Above all there was a new sense of nationhood, due largely to the Prussian minister Bismarck's unification of German states in 1871. This was the Second Reich or Empire. The First had been the so-called Holy Roman Empire of the German nation, which Napoleon had destroyed. With Bismarck's unification came a new pride and a desire to demonstrate that Germany was equal to or better than other European nations.

At the same time, there was dissatisfaction among workers in factories and coal-mines, just as there was in every industrialised country. The Social Democrat Party, including what we would now call both Socialists and Communists, grew fast, and although it was suppressed for a time it became one of the most numerous of its kind in Europe.

After dismissing Bismarck in 1890, the new Emperor, the young Wilhelm II, began to adopt a new policy. He was a vain man, fond of dressing up and giving parties in which he would appear as his warlike predecessor Frederick the Great. This vanity was to have disastrous consequences. Wilhelm acquired colonies for Germany, though Bismarck had advised him not to. He threatened Britain by trying to rival her navy, and in 1911 he almost went to war with France.

Yet Germany had been known for many years as a peaceful nation, the 'land of poets and thinkers'. Goethe and Schiller in literature, Bach, Beethoven, Wagner and Brahms in music, had been among the chief figures in a late Renaissance of culture which rivalled Italy's in the fifteenth and sixteenth centuries. The new military mood of the Second Reich gave no inkling at the time of the catastrophe which was to come in the years from 1933 to 1945.

The Great War

Wilhelm's swashbuckling was not by any means the sole cause of the war. There were other causes: fear that Germany and Austria were encircled by enemies; rival nationalisms; and Austria's threat to Serbia, which led directly to war between Austria and Russia. Germany, as Austria's ally, declared war on Russia on 1 August 1914, and on France two days later; Britain intervened on 4 August, and there began the most widespread war in the history of mankind till that date.

On all sides, it was expected that the war would soon be over. Like many British people, Germans of all parties were excited at the prospect of glory. Even the Socialists, who had sworn never to fight against their fellow-workers abroad, joined with enthusiasm in what seemed to them a war against Socialism's chief opponent, the Tsar of Russia. They believed too that the war was a sign that the system of private ownership of business, capitalism, was breaking down, and that the time of revolution was close at hand.

The plan of the German General Staff was to defeat France in six weeks and Russia in six months, leaving Britain isolated. The plan met disaster at the battle of the Marne, in September 1914, when the French held the German advance. Then began the four-years' struggle which gained almost no territory for either side. Though the German armies were most successful against Russia, in Belgium and France they were forced to dig trenches which stretched from the English Channel to the Swiss Alps. The area between the opposing armies was a quagmire. Soldiers were killed by the million. Food ran short, and in 1917 there was a mutiny in the German navy. Though the Russian Revolution of October 1917 led to the withdrawal from the war of Germany's most numerous opponent, the entry of the USA in April that same year had left the Germans little hope. On 29 September 1918, after a last effort by Field-Marshal Ludendorff, the High Command advised Emperor Wilhelm that Germany must ask for peace. Even so, it was not until 11 November that an armistice was signed, and by that time the Emperor had fled. The Social Democrats,

who had been left to form a government, had to carry the humiliation of defeat.

Revolution

Throughout Europe, the end of the war brought upheavals which seemed to need a strong hand to control them. The Bolshevik revolution in Russia had been most thoroughgoing. For a time it seemed that all power had been seized by the people, and that a new dawn had begun for mankind. But the Russians, under the increasingly dictatorial leadership of Lenin, horrified the rest of Europe by their ruthless policies. In the next few years after 1917 hundreds of thousands, perhaps millions, of men and women thought to be anti-Communist were put to death or exiled in Siberia. As a result, in Germany, the Social Democrats became divided. The more extreme group, those who wanted to follow the Russian example, attempted a revolution in Berlin almost as soon as the armistice had been signed. These Spartacists, named after Spartacus, the leader of a Roman slave revolt, had little success, though a flicker of gunfire continued in the capital for some months. The Communist Party of Germany, which derived from the Spartacists and was founded in 1919, received a severe setback when its leaders, Karl Liebknecht and Rosa Luxemburg, were assassinated by right-wing opponents. In Bavaria, too, the Communists were defeated. In the former capital of Bavaria, Munich, there was for a few months in 1919 a soviet, or workers' council, on the lines of those in Russia. But this was put down by bands of armed ex-soldiers, the so-called Freikorps, who detested Socialism and Communism as signs of degeneracy. When the year 1919 ended, some thought that not only had Communism and Socialism been frustrated, but that the newly proclaimed Republic was hand-in-glove with the militarists who had been dominant in Wilhelm II's time.

Humiliation

After forty-seven years of unity, the only effective unity Germany had known in the whole of its history, Germans suddenly found themselves humiliated and hated. To the victors, they seemed to have become regimented monsters. Many stories were told of the atrocities German soldiers had committed, not all true. The millions of deaths and the damage to property caused by the war were laid at their door, and they were expected to pay for it all. As the British politician Sir Eric Geddes said in 1918, 'They are going to be squeezed, as a lemon is squeezed – until the pips squeak.'

Such vindictive ideas were not the only motives of the Allies who signed the Treaty of Versailles of 1919, though they were later made to appear so. The German leaders signed under protest. They admitted, against their will, German guilt in causing the war; they gave up German-speaking territories such as Alsace-Lorraine; they granted the French the right to occupy the left bank of the Rhine; they allowed East Prussia to be cut off from the rest of Germany by a Polish 'corridor' (which gave Poland access to the sea), and they allowed Danzig on the Baltic Sea to become a 'free city'. They also agreed to pay the huge reparations about which Geddes had joked, to give up all colonies, and to reduce the armed forces to a minimum.

Germany in the 1920s
Lost by Germany 1919
Saar: League of Nations control 1919–35
Demilitarised Rhineland 1919–36
0 ———— 300 km
0 ———— 200 miles

To many Germans this appeared, both at the time and later, to be a treaty dictated by revenge. In order to pay reparations they needed the factories which were being dismantled, and the food which they were prevented from buying abroad. They felt they were being crushed because they had become too powerful a commercial rival. Feelings of this kind led a few years later to support for nationalist movements which might not otherwise have been given.

Yet with all allowance made for German resentment at the Treaty of Versailles, it must be said that a warlike spirit had been fostered in Germany before 1914 in a reckless way: war was a test of manhood; peace encouraged effeminate sloth; a country like Germany had to go to war to prove it was no weakling. Such ideas, often ascribed to the philosopher Friedrich Nietzsche and his English disciple Houston Stewart Chamberlain, who hated England, were spread about, even by some of Germany's greatest writers, and other nations assumed they had been deliberately put into practice. Besides, Germany, fearing Bolshevism, had forced Russia to give up even more at the Treaty of Brest-Litovsk in 1918. Germany was wronged in 1919, but that did not put her in the right.

2 The rise of the Weimar Republic

After the First World War German money became almost valueless. This grocer photographed in 1922 has no room in his till for all the banknotes he receives, and has to keep them in a large chest.

On 11 August 1919 a new constitution was set up for Germany, the first article of which explicitly announced, 'The power of the State derives from the people.'

This was a spirit entirely new to Germany as a whole. For the first time, a real parliamentary democracy was created, with votes for all men and women over twenty (not at that time granted in Britain) secret ballots, and a government which had to seek re-election every four years. The Weimar Republic, named after the town of the poet Goethe, the representative of tolerant humanity, and of his close friend Schiller, had the most liberal régime of any in Europe. Some said it was too liberal. The parties represented in it were so numerous – more than twenty in all – that it was difficult for any one of them to put a programme into action, though the Social Democrats were the strongest, with nearly a quarter of the total number of seats during almost the whole life of the Republic. Others of only slightly smaller size were the Zentrum (Centre) for which Catholics usually voted, and the Communist Party, which increased from 4 seats in 1920 to 77 in 1930. Hitler's party, the National Socialists, was founded in 1920. Both the Communists and the National Socialists wanted to overthrow the tolerant parliamentary system of the Weimar Republic, and the Weimar Constitution guaranteed their right to spread their ideas and arguments.

Unfortunately there was one article which, intended to preserve the Republic in time of danger, gave to the President in an emergency all power, including military. This was later used by Hitler to destroy the Republic.

The years of poverty and shame

Despite defeat, the war had seemed to some Germans to have been the start of a great renewal. The disaster had been necessary so that a new mankind could arise from it; many plays and poems dwelled on this theme. In reality, the post-war years were almost as bad as the war itself, as far as living conditions for civilians went. People in towns lived on starvation rations, although country people usually had eggs and butter, bread and meat, for which they charged high prices. Money came to be worth less and less. Farmers were soon not much interested in supposedly valuable paper money, and demanded instead family heirlooms, grandfather's watch, a wedding ring, any object which would keep its value. Workers had to be paid daily, and bought their food at once, before another rise in prices next day destroyed the value of what they had earned. By 1923 wages were paid in millions of marks and it was necessary to pay millions for quite ordinary things. The story goes that some people papered their walls with banknotes instead of wallpaper – it was cheaper. Saving money was useless, and anyone depending on a fixed pension was in a desperate position. People who had been prudent and saved money were hard hit.

On 19 January 1924 the German Government ordered passive resistance to the French troops occupying the Ruhr. In this poster a German miner, threatened by French soldiers, says 'No! I will not be forced.'

Adding to this humiliation, the French took advantage of the failure of Germany to keep up to date with reparations payments, and in 1923 their troops occupied the industrial area of the Ruhr. This was particularly resented, not merely because French troops tried to force German workers to work harder, but because some of the troops were black Senegalese. In the conditions of the time, this was deliberately insulting.

New nationalism

Throughout Europe in the post-war years there was an increase in nationalism, which often led to dictatorships. In Italy, Mussolini became Prime Minister in 1922 and set up a so-called corporate state controlled by his Fascist Party, which was both nationalistic and, in a sense, Socialist. He looked to the great past of the Roman Empire for inspiration and he organised the nation in groups of workers in all fields, forcing them to co-operate in a common cause. In Russia, the originally international nature of Communism was increasingly changed by Stalin after 1928 through a policy of 'Socialism in one country'. Dictatorships were set up in Hungary, Bulgaria,

Greece. In many parts of Europe parliamentary democracy, which had scarcely begun to show its face, was declared incompetent. Even in England, in the early 1930s, the British Union of Fascists set up by Sir Oswald Mosley was modelled on Mussolini's Fascists.

In Germany there was a long tradition, going back to the late eighteenth century, which maintained, as the philosopher Adam Müller said, that 'all that is great and deep and permanent in European institutions is German'. This was an 'anti-Western' belief, opposed to democracy, and partly favourable to Russia and in favour of mystical introspection. It came to mean eventually that all Europe, or even the world, must become German. By the early 1920s it had gained in strength through the very fact that German imperial nationalism had been defeated. Military men in particular, who had been worshipped as heroes in Wilhelm II's time, disliked the atmosphere of the Weimar Republic. Some of them joined the Freikorps. Nearly all of them refused to believe that the German armies had been defeated in 1918, though that was the plain fact of the matter. They preferred to think that they had been 'stabbed in the back' by pacifistic Socialists at home. Socialism, moreover, they maintained was a Jewish invention, and these people usually despised Jews. Such men were ready recruits for the German Workers' Party, which Hitler joined on 16 October 1919, and which shortly afterwards added the words 'National Socialist' to its name. This was the party later known as 'the Nazis'. It was still very small, but Hitler was to transform it in the next fourteen years into the only party in Germany with any right to exist.

Hitler's early years

Adolf Hitler was born on 20 April 1889 in the Austrian frontier town of Braunau on the Inn, only about 100 kilometres (60 miles) from Munich. By his own account he had a hard time in his youth, fighting against the odds to establish himself as a genius, but research does not bear this out. He was not rich, but not poverty-stricken either. The reasons for his failure to pass his school examinations (he failed in German language, among other things) did not lie in his upbringing. Nor did he lack support when he moved as a young man to Vienna, for his widowed mother provided him with money enough. He failed at everything he tried. After the

Vienna Academy of Art had twice rejected him as a painter, he spent his time trying to sell his pictures, going to the opera, and reading magazines which glorified the Germanic past, preached the doctrine of the German 'master-race', and blamed Germany's misfortunes on the Jews. For several years after he reached the age of twenty, he disappeared from society; it is clear now that he must have been escaping military service in the Austrian army.

In 1914 Hitler volunteered for the German army. He served for four years mainly as a messenger at regimental headquarters, was wounded several times, and won the Iron Cross First Class, for bravery. This was an unusual distinction for a corporal. He learned of Germany's defeat while recovering in the hospital from being gassed. But the end of the war did not make him decide at once to restore the national fortunes, as he claimed. He remained in the army through the worst period of the post-war months, although he could have been demobilised immediately. He emerged into civilian life still uncertain about his purpose. After he had joined the German Workers' Party, it is true, his life gained a certain direction. But his first attempt at gaining power in the inglorious Munich *putsch* of 9 November 1923 was a half-hearted one. After announcing that he intended to overthrow the government, he led, with Field-Marshal Ludendorff, a column of perhaps two thousand men through the streets of Munich, but when the police opened fire he hurled himself to the ground so hard that he put his shoulder out of joint. His later attempts to turn this incident into a heroic adventure were exaggerations.

Arrested soon afterwards, Hitler was sentenced by a sympathetic court—judges tended at that time to favour men like him—to five years' detention in the fortress at Landsberg, where he spent in fact less than a year in fairly comfortable surroundings and was able to write the first part of his book *Mein Kampf* (My Struggle).

This book, later presented to every German couple at their wedding as though it were a kind of Bible, is a shapeless, ungrammatical muddle of rhetorical tirades on a small group of themes—nationalism, racist and anti-democratic theories—and announcements of future actions. These last are the parts in which Hitler was most at home. He describes with cynical frankness how he intends to manipulate the masses by means of propaganda, insisting always that might is right, and forecasting a worldwide battle for racial superiority. Germany is to

be freed of all limitations imposed by the Treaty of Versailles. An assault on Russia is to be made to destroy Communism or, as he prefers to call it, Bolshevism. And the Jews are to be frustrated in their international plan to bleed the German people to death. There was no secret about this programme. Though he later dismissed what he had written as merely 'fantasies behind bars,' in the next twenty years Hitler put it all into action.

Emerging from his captivity in December 1924, Hitler was now a martyr for the cause. Though his party had been outlawed, his task was to reorganise it.

Weimar succeeds

The first real German democracy was beginning, by 1924, to assert itself. The heavy responsibility of paying reparations was lightened by the Dawes Plan, named after the American statesman who organised it. The Allies now realised that if Germany's economy collapsed it would probably upset their own economies; the industrialised nations were too closely connected by trade and finance for one to fall without damaging the rest. So they enabled Germany to balance her budget, and a new gold currency was introduced to replace the now almost useless paper money. Released from the chaos of inflation, the Germans began to work with a new zest. Within a few years prosperity seemed within reach. The Foreign Minister Stresemann succeeded in 1926, against Russian opposition, in having Germany admitted as a member of the League of Nations, roughly the equivalent of the United Nations Organisation of today, and signed in 1925 the Locarno Agreements, a series of non-aggression pacts which earned him the Nobel Peace Prize. Though most foreign diplomats were aware that Stresemann was a fervent nationalist, the acceptance of Germany once more as one of the leading nations of Europe was a step which all welcomed. True, the presidential elections of 1925 brought into office Field-Marshal Hindenburg, the hero of the imperial army and a firm believer in the 'stab-in-the-back' theory. In addition, the 'patriotic' parties were able to argue that the new internationalism and acceptance of outside help was further evidence of Jewish trickery. But the Republic began to make its mark, and not only in the political and economic fields.

In the brief thirteen years of its existence, the Weimar Republic was creative in every branch of the arts and sciences. Its new cinema industry was the only one in the world, except the Russian, to concentrate on serious films, which are still shown today. In music, there were not only such composers as Paul Hindemith and Kurt Weill, but magnificent orchestras like the Berlin Philharmonic, famous conductors such as Bruno Walter and Wilhelm Furtwängler. No less famous were the scientists Albert Einstein and Max Planck. The university of Göttingen was one of the greatest scientific centres in the world. Painters such as Oskar Kokoschka, Paul Klee and Wassily Kandinsky, and the school of art and architecture founded by Walter Gropius, the Bauhaus, gained international recognition. Though the night-shows and sexual licence of Berlin's West End were pointed to as marks of decadence, there were many signs of a healthy intellectual and artistic life.

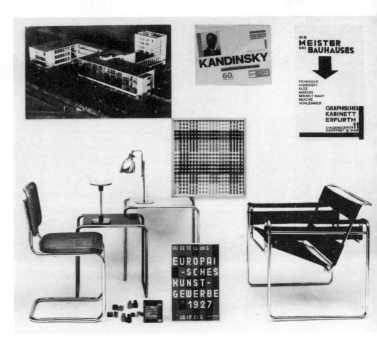

This display shows furniture and graphic work designed at the Bauhaus in the 1920s, also a photograph of this important school of art and architecture. The Bauhaus movement was suppressed when Hitler came to power and some of the people who had worked there were forced into exile. The influence of the Bauhaus on modern design was strong.

People still argue whether the Republic showed too much tolerance. Some say that Germans had had too little experience of freedom to know how to manage it. There was no strong tradition of reasonableness and self-restraint, rather a tradition of flying to extremes. To add to the difficulties, many believed in philosophies which were based on the idea of contradictory extremes: Marxists, Nazis, followers of Nietzsche were all alike in supposing that man can only 'think in opposites', and in supposing that they could act 'beyond good and evil'. They looked down on compromises, middle paths between extremes, and careful balancing of differing demands. They were ready to kill opponents not because it was right but because morality was over and done with. The result was a harsh intolerance, the very thing that the Weimar Constitution was meant to get rid of, and an arrogant cruelty, though many other Germans were reasonable and peaceful.

3 Economic crisis and Nazi takeover

The Wall Street crash

Germany had scarcely found its feet again when a financial crisis undid almost all that had been achieved. In October 1929, people with money invested in American industry suddenly lost confidence – nobody really knows why – and began to sell their shares. The price of shares fell and others took fright and sold their own shares before it was too late. Many American businesses and industries collapsed, and because they were so important for international trade, every industrial country in the world was affected.

Germany was at least as hard hit as the rest. This 'Wall Street crash', named after the street in New York where shares are bought and sold, threw millions of Germans out of work. By February 1931 the number of unemployed was almost 5 million, a year later it was well over 6 million. The Communists said that this was just what they had predicted: capitalism was entering one of its crises which must soon end in its self-destruction. The National Socialists were delighted that Jewish finance, as they called it, had come so close to total disaster.

Both Communists and National Socialists argued, as they had done all along, that democracy was also showing its fatal weaknesses. A dictatorship was necessary, they said. But though they agreed on this, the Communists and National Socialists were bitter enemies. They set up rival armies of volunteers, who engaged in street-fighting while the more peaceable parties stood by, without a remedy.

Chancellor Brüning, appointed in 1930, tried the same measures as those being used in other countries: heavy taxation, reductions in wages and a Price Commission to keep down the cost of goods in the shops. Though the wisdom of his policy has been disputed, he claimed that by the spring of 1932 he had almost succeeded. But by then he was on the point of being dismissed, partly because some influential politicians

A photomontage by 'John Heartfield' (Wieland Herzfelde) from a cover of a magazine of 1932. The German reads: 'The meaning of the Hitler-salute'; 'Millions are backing me'; 'A little man asks for great gifts'. The millions, the picture implies, are the millions provided by capitalist sympathisers, not millions of people, as Hitler meant.

believed that the time had come to reach an understanding with the Nazis. The Nazi Party had in fact surprised everyone by its success in the parliamentary elections of 1930, when it increased its votes from 800,000 in 1928 to over 6 million, in comparison with 8 million Social Democrat, 4 million Zentrum, and 4 million Communist votes. With 107 seats in the Reichstag, or parliament, the Nazis were now second only to the Social Democrats.

How the Nazis gained support

Gaining almost one fifth of the votes cast in 1930 was achieved by clever tactics. Two years earlier, the Nazis had been a very small party. With the financial help of the millionaire Fritz Thyssen and others, especially Alfred Hugenberg, who owned a chain of newspapers, a news agency, and a film company, and who detested the democratic Republic, the spreading of political propaganda had become much easier. It was simple to play on the anxiety caused by the Wall Street crash and revive resentment against the Treaty of Versailles and other grievances. But the Nazis also got inside organisations such as the students' unions, provoking university authorities to over-react, and thus gaining sympathy from students. They organised impressive mass-meetings, especially at Nuremberg, a city with medieval associations and strongly 'Germanic' buildings and fortifications. Seeing thousands of Hitler's followers in their brown shirts, breeches and jackboots (the so-called *Sturm-Abteilung* (SA), or Stormtroopers) and the columns of *Hitler Jugend* (Hitler Youth) marching through the town, Germans were given the impression, as early as 1929, that the Nazis were numerically much stronger than they really were.

Supporting the Nazis could often seem quite reasonable. Though they themselves were violent, this could be represented as a manly defence against Communists, and it was easy to play upon the frightening memory of the bloodshed in the Bolshevik revolution. The Nazi propaganda office promoted pride in German achievements before the war and blamed the Jews for Germany's troubles. The fact that Jews did control very many businesses was undeniable, though it did not follow that these firms were conducted against German interests. Nor did Germans who accepted such arguments at face value necessarily agree with the rest of the Nazi case, that Jews and capitalists were one and the same, that Jews were filthy 'in their blood', infecting the generous, innocent, loving race of pure Germans. At its extreme, this

'National race for SA'. In this poster a Stormtrooper in SA uniform strides out heroically, saluted by young people, though a priest wrings his hands and a capitalist tries to hold him back. (According to Communists, the Nazis were being helped by capitalists; the Nazis, however, claimed to be Socialists.)

attitude, called anti-Semitism, took the form of demanding the extermination of the Jews. 'Juda Verrecke!' was the slogan which appeared everywhere. In the same way English Fascists used to write on the walls of London in the 1930s 'P.J.,' 'Perish Judah.' But this could always be explained away to moderates as the view of a minority which had to be allowed for in accepting the much larger programme (abolition of unemployment, a housing policy, restoration of German greatness) which Nazism offered.

In any case, opposition was difficult at the many mass meetings where Hitler now spoke. First, he could always count on some approval of his arguments. Some members of the audience might think of at least one Jew who could be suspected of cheating them, or remember one family which had been starved by the British after the war, or one brave German soldier who had sacrificed his life, or one occasion when several Communists had beaten up a Nazi. 'Proving' a point by giving only one example of what you claim to be generally true is the method of the demagogue. And if there should be any heckling at these meetings, it was soon silenced. The heckler would be hauled out of his seat by two or three Stormtroopers, dragged out of the hall by his hair, kicked in the face, and thrown down the stairs outside. Those who remained were not only shocked but as though hypnotised. They would, at the end, rise from their seats with thundering shouts of 'Sieg Heil!,' 'Victory, Hail!'.

Events of 1932

When Brüning ceased to be Chancellor, his place was taken by von Papen, a man of the Zentrum, but opposed to party government. He was much more inclined to collaborate for his own ends with Hitler, and lacked Brüning's desire to rescue parliamentary democracy. Papen's first concession to the Nazis was to dissolve the new Reichstag before it had even met; this was on 4 June 1932. It meant a new election and a state of uncertainty in the country. Two weeks later he removed the prohibition against the Stormtroopers wearing uniform, agreed upon only a short while before. His third action was to attempt, on 20 July, to override the largest state in Germany, Socialist-dominated Prussia, where Stormtroopers had been forbidden since 1930. In this he was astonishingly successful. He sent a lieutenant and ten men to depose the Social Democrats, and the Prussians respectfully gave way.

The flood-gates were now open. Papen's hopes that he could win over the Nazis were vain. The lifting of the ban on the Stormtroopers led merely to more violence, and caused many deaths. Social Democrats, used to acting within the law, saw the government itself betraying them. The Communists had instructions from Stalin to treat all non-Communists as enemies, so the Left was divided. At the Reichstag elections of 31 July Hitler's party received nearly 14 million votes (still not a majority of the total votes cast), and became the strongest single party, with 230 seats. President Hindenburg, however, was not yet prepared to accept the upstart Hitler—a former corporal—as Chancellor, and Hitler was not prepared to accept any lesser position. This was a risky course for Hitler: Papen called yet another Reichstag election, in which the Nazi vote fell for the first time. Yet Papen had lost the confidence of his own supporters, and on 2 December von Schleicher took over as Chancellor. He too was unsuccessful. By 30 January 1933, Hitler had achieved what he was holding out for, and had become Chancellor of the Reich himself, under Hindenburg's Presidency. Yet at no time up to this point had his party ever received a majority of the votes cast at any election.

Gaining complete control

The months after Hitler became Chancellor were often described by the Nazis as a 'bloodless' or a 'legal' revolution, in the sense that, unlike the French and the Russian revolutions, they did not involve thousands of deaths. There was some truth in this, though it concealed the terrorism which made it often unnecessary to go as far as executions. Concentration camps, which were not the same as the later extermination camps, existed at Oranienburg and Dachau as early as 1933, and the 're-education' in them of opponents of the Nazis, which often involved forced labour for men entirely unused to it, could result in death. Stormtroopers stood outside Jewish shops defying customers to enter. In Chemnitz, a member of parliament was forced into an open cart, and two fellow Social Democrats were compelled by threats to drag him round the town. Opponents were flogged with rubber truncheons, sometimes tied in sacks and thrown into rivers. But many people did not hear about events like these. The newspapers and radio were soon under Nazi control. They made public only those items of news which suited them.

Hitler took three 'legal' measures. First, on 1 February 1933 he obtained President Hindenburg's consent to dissolve

Hitler posing in 1933 with a carefully mounted crowd of admirers.

the Reichstag once again. For the next seven weeks, he governed by emergency decrees (thanks to the article in the Constitution which allowed this). He restricted the freedom of the press and expression of opinion, brought Social Democratic Prussia finally into line, suspended the basic rights of individuals guaranteed by the Weimar Constitution, and forced all other *Lands* of Germany to accept Nazi officials. Then followed, on 27 February, a fire which destroyed the Reichstag building. Hitler blamed the Communists. Then, having aroused the fears of a large majority, he declared a general election for 5 March. Astonishingly, even with all this preparation the Nazis polled only 43·9% of the votes, while the Left-wing Socialist parties, even though many of their candidates had been persecuted or imprisoned, still polled 30%.

This victory was still quite legal, but it was clearly not enough for Hitler's purposes. The election gave him a right to govern only with the help of another party, together with which he could build a majority. He therefore, as his second measure, passed the 'Enabling Act' of 23 March 1933. This effectively ended the powers of the Reichstag, and went on to liquidate all that remained of the democratic State. The civil service and the judiciary were 'cleansed' of unwanted officials. The trades unions were embodied in a single National Socialist 'German Labour Front', and on 14 July all non-Nazi parties were dissolved. The third measure was the alliance of the Party with the army, and subordination of the police to the black-uniformed *Schutzstaffeln* (SS), or security squads, originally Hitler's private bodyguard.

Resistance was weak. Many businessmen, high-ranking officers, and even some churchmen were actively in favour of Hitler, believing he could be made use of. Bureaucrats had had obedience ingrained for generations. The trades unions gave in without a murmur, after SS and Stormtroopers had taken their offices by force. The youth organisations, such as the Boy Scouts, which were 'railroaded' (*gleichgeschaltet*) into the Hitler Youth, also made no protest. But then neither did the rest of the world, at that time. The Vatican, which had never signed a concordat with the Weimar Republic, did so with Hitler's régime within six months of his taking power. Fear of atheist Communism, and the hope of preserving some rights for Catholic priests, were the Pope's chief motives. A similar fear of Communism soon prompted the prime ministers of Britain and France to allow Hitler to go on without interference, though some people urged them to take action against an apparently still defenceless Germany where so much barbarism was being openly practised.

By the end of 1933, Hitler had replaced elections with plebiscites in which the choice offered was only that of saying 'Yes' or 'No' to the new régime. Officially, 87·8% voted 'Yes' in November that year, and though in some parts of Berlin the percentage was as low as two thirds, it seemed outwardly, at least, that almost the whole nation was united behind its leader. After Hindenburg had died in 1934, Hitler did not appoint himself President. Instead he made himself head of the German State with the new title of 'Führer', leader.

4 The Third Reich

The Nazi State

Germany was now ruled in accordance with the 'leadership principle', giving power to 'leaders' who owed obedience only to *the* Leader, Hitler, himself. As the slogan put it, 'Germany is Hitler, and Hitler is Germany.'

This identification of a country with its ruler was a new idea of government, though it had been described in the early nineteenth century by the philosopher Hegel as the typical principle in countries ruled by 'men of world-history' – Napoleon, Julius Caesar, Alexander the Great. Hitler did see himself, it is true, as a new Caesar. His legions of Stormtroopers carried standards like Roman legionaries; the raised arm of the 'Hitler salute' imitated the Roman form of greeting; Nazi architecture imitated the Roman, and the expectation that the régime would be a 'thousand-year Reich' was based on the Holy Roman Empire, founded by Charlemagne in AD 800, which lasted just over a thousand years.

Contradictorily, Hitler also declared, 'The Party is now the State'. Since only a small proportion of Germans were actually Party members, it followed that many Germans were not identified with Hitler. In addition, the civil service was soon gathering as much power into its own hands as possible, rather than let the Party acquire it. But though the logic was faulty, the 'leader principle' was put into operation by selecting efficient Party-members for schooling as an élite. They would implement new policies, while the State would continue the traditional forms of administration. Party and State, or government, were thus liable to be at variance. When the concept of 'the people' was added to this, as one more factor in the constitution, the position became yet more obscure. In practice, the Leader made decisions at top level, and these were implemented or not according to circumstances. There was no programme that had been debated and voted upon, and which the Leader was morally bound to adopt.

A Nazi Party rally in 1935. The eagle standards are like the ones carried by Roman legionaries, and the row of arches at the far end looks slightly Roman. Hitler stands alone facing thousands of people in the arena, all in disciplined rows.

Germany was now divided into *Gauen*, an old word meaning regions, each under a *Gauleiter*, who was supposed to give commands in the name of the Party to 'the State' in his area. It was an inefficient way of governing, since few policies were properly defined, and there was a temptation for each official to play for an increase in his own power. As this led to disputes, in the end the arrangement played into Hitler's hands. In any difficult situation he was able to hold back, and only take sides when he saw advantage for himself in maintaining his dictatorial position.

The racial creed

England had driven out the Jews almost completely from 1290 to the middle of the seventeenth century, and even then kept them under disadvantages: they could not enter Parliament or attend universities for roughly another two hundred years. In Germany, Jews had congregated ever since the early Middle Ages, especially in large cities like Frankfurt, where even in the nineteenth century some of them lived segregated in a special district known as a ghetto and were not allowed to celebrate more than a small number of marriages each year. This led to their being looked upon as secretive and mysterious, especially when they maintained their ancient dress and religious customs. As they were not allowed to work on the land, they were often money-lenders, charging interest which was believed, in the Middle Ages, to be sinful. In the Middle Ages also, the Church often recalled the Jews' supposed responsibility for the death of Christ, and persecutions resulted. Stories circulated and persisted, wrongly, even into the twentieth century, that Jews killed Christian children as part of their ritual ceremonies.

On the other hand, Jewish families like the Rothschilds in the eighteenth and nineteenth centuries acquired very great fortunes and were able to use their money politically. Bismarck could not have carried out some of his policies without the help of a Jewish financier who supplied him with money which the Reichstag denied him. These well-known instances of Jewish power gave a little colour to the idea that an international organisation existed, whose purpose was to control the whole of Germany.

The increasing tolerance of Jews from the eighteenth century onwards brought more of them into Germany, and this

Another photomontage, published in May 1934, by 'John Heartfield' (see p. 11) 'As in the Middle Ages, so in the Third Reich'. A man is shown pinned down by the swastika beneath a medieval sculpture of a man being tortured on the wheel.

quickly revived old fears. The most lurid document against the Jews was the *Protocols of the Elders of Zion*, supposed to be the record of a meeting held in 1897. Published in Russia, it gave rise there to *pogroms*, or mass attacks on Jews, which the Nazis were to imitate. There was already, however, a mistaken but pseudo-scientific theory which had for many years tried to show that the Jews were racially inferior to the so-called Aryan race. 'Aryan' is properly applied to the languages of Europe, India and Iran which belong to the Indo-European group of languages, though the Nazis used it to distinguish the supposedly superior Nordic races, including first and foremost the Germans. Many nineteenth-century writers, including Joseph Gobineau and Dühring, believed in these doctrines. Nietzsche, though he attacked Richard Wagner for his anti-Semitism, blamed the Jewish race for crippling strong leaders with guilty feelings which hindered them from acting boldly. There were small anti-Jewish parties in Bismarck's Reichstag. None of them was as thoroughgoing as the Nazis in the Third Reich.

Jews were now publicly humiliated. On one occasion Stormtroopers stopped a young Jew and cut the pattern of their symbol, the swastika, into his hair. Jewish shops were boycotted in 1933 throughout Germany for one whole day. Stickers appeared on shop windows reading 'Jews not wanted here'. More important, the Nuremberg Laws of September 1935, which, grotesquely enough, had been sketched out on old menu-cards in a beer-hall only a few hours before they were passed, declared that 'those of non-German blood' had no civil rights. Marriages between Germans and Jews were forbidden; sexual relations between Germans and Jews were punishable with hard labour (and from 1939 onwards with death). Anybody with one Jewish grandparent was defined as a Jew. Such harassing of millions of citizens was already a step towards the policy of extermination that was to come.

Hitler and Himmler, head of the SS, inspecting an SS guard of honour.

The rule of the SS

Hitler had secured his own position in the party after his release from Landsberg in 1924 by creating the SS as his personal bodyguard. These black-uniformed troops with their skull-and-crossbones badge, selected for their devotion to Hitler and for the proven 'purity' of their blood since 1750, became after 1933 increasingly powerful. They were an élite which rivalled the traditional élite of the German army officer corps as well as the Stormtroopers, and which gradually gained the upper hand. The leader of the SS from 1929 onwards was Heinrich Himmler, a man described by an Australian visitor in 1936 as 'much kindlier and more thoughtful for his guests than any other Nazi leader, a man of exquisite courtesy …' Yet this deceptive appearance, calculated to deceive Germans too, was the mask of a man who rose to power only after Hitler had ordered the murder of his rival, the Stormtroopers' leader Ernst Röhm and 200 of his associates, in the so-called 'Night of the Long Knives' in 1934. He was a man who later displayed unparalleled cruelty.

Himmler extended his control rapidly: in 1935 he was chief of the political police, in 1936 chief of all police; in 1943 he combined this post with the Ministry of the Interior. Once the 'SS state' was created, resistance was dangerous as never before. Special branches of the SS were created with the task of destroying or disrupting all Marxist groups, churches, sects, emigrants, Jews, as well as preventing homosexuality and abortion. The *Geheime Staatspolizei* (Gestapo), or secret police, infiltrated organisations, and used torture when questioning suspects. The ordinary police were increasingly made to fit into the same organisation, so that a network of spies and detectives was created to deal with everything of which Hitler disapproved. Crime and membership of a 'non-Aryan' race or an anti-Nazi group became indistinguishable.

The SS were responsible for setting up the new concentration camps of various kinds which now appeared all over Germany. A man suspected of disloyalty or opposition might first be treated indulgently, as the well-known writer Ernst Wiechert was: a furnished room with private meals and frequent visitors could be provided. Without warning, he might then find himself, as Wiechert did, transferred to a camp where the first thing he saw was a man strung up on a wooden frame, undergoing a flogging. Then followed hard labour, hacking stones and carrying them long distances without proper equipment. The slightest sign of delay or disobedience brought harsh punishment. Newcomers to the camp could expect, in any case, to be thrashed the first night, while they were trying to sleep.

Though the SS were intended to ensure uniformity, their special position as a kind of state-within-the-state often produced conflict. Their military intelligence service competed with that of the armed forces, sometimes working in opposition to it. Like the Gauleiters and the civil service, they created divisions where none were supposed to exist.

Why did the Germans support Hitler?

In the early days after 30 January 1933 many Germans were ready to believe that the brutality of the Nazis was only a minor fault, which Hitler would correct. He promoted this idea by having himself photographed, for instance, stooping to pat on the cheek a small girl who was presenting him with a bouquet. A popular postcard on sale everywhere showed him wearing white armour, riding into battle for good against evil, like a Sir Galahad. His propaganda machine put out blatant lies, which a moment's reflection would show to be untrue. 'Any idiot can rule with a rubber truncheon', were the words of an official poster in Frankfurt in 1938, implying that the Nazis never used such means. This was a fine example of the principle announced by the Minister of Propaganda, Josef Goebbels, that the bigger the lie, the more people are willing to believe it. It is an extension of the idea 'no smoke without fire', and this method meant creating as much smoke as possible.

Many Germans may have been sceptical. But there were subtle ways in which an impression could be created that the whole nation was really in favour of the Nazis. The film of one of the annual mass-rallies at Nuremberg, *The Triumph of the Will*, shows how rank on rank of Stormtroopers are applauded, as they march past, by Germans wearing traditional costumes. Hitler himself descends out of the clouds in his private airliner, like a god from Valhalla, and is hailed on all sides. Young men from all parts of Germany solemnly call out the names of the provinces they represent. At the end of the film, the entire nation seems to embody the slogan 'Ein Volk, ein Reich, ein Führer' (One People, One Reich, One Leader).

On a smaller scale, people were kept in line by the *Blocklei-*

Hitler at his mountain home in the Bavarian mountains near Berchtesgaden, probably in 1937, demonstrating his love of children. The boy in the middle of the row is standing to attention in military style.

ter, a Party member responsible for a very small area. If you happened to omit the greeting 'Heil Hitler!' when you met him, there would be serious consequences. To avoid these, you would perhaps say 'Heil Hitler!' even when it was unnecessary, and so give others the impression that you yourself were a keen supporter. Your children, as members of the 'Hitler Youth', were expected to report anything their parents might say against the government. In this way, almost everyone got into the habit of behaving outwardly as a loyal Nazi.

Here and there, a protest would be made. In 1937 Pope Pius XI issued a message, 'Mit brennender Sorge' (With deep concern), warning the Catholic clergy. Protestants, inspired by Bishop Dibelius and Pastor Niemöller, spoke out. The Jewish-born Carmelite nun Edith Stein replied to a Gestapo man's 'Heil Hitler' with 'Laudetur Jesus Christus' (Praised be Jesus Christ). She escaped retribution for a short while, though a few years later she died in a gas-chamber at Auschwitz. But to act in that way needed exceptional courage.

above: *The German Olympic Games Committee arriving at London to advertise the Games held in Berlin in 1936. The Nazis used the Games to get recognition abroad. They used civil planes like this Junkers 52 for training bomber pilots, and for bombing in Spain during the Civil War.*

above left: *The launching of the battleship 'Scharnhorst' at Wilhelmshaven, 3 October 1936. The 'Hitler salute' is being given on all sides. This ship was expected to be a 'pocket battleship' of 10,000 tons, but proved to be of 26,000 tons and of a new, much more formidable design.*

Hitler brings back prosperity

A further reason for supporting Hitler was that he put a stop to unemployment. Admittedly there were new uniforms to be made by the thousand, and the new motorways, among the first in Europe, could serve military as well as civilian purposes, but there were also large-scale housing schemes. Hitler started a travel agency called 'Strength Through Joy', which provided for members of the Party very cheap holidays: cruises, seaside hotels, camps in the mountains. He set up the 'Winter Aid Charity', which meant that around Christmas you would get a knock on the door from a smiling Party member and a polite request to put something in the box for old people. After thirteen years of the Weimar Republic, only four or five of which had shown signs of bringing back prosperity, and which had ended with mass unemployment, the new régime was warmly welcome.

The new armament programme also reduced unemployment. Under the Treaty of Versailles, the German army had been limited to 100,000 men, and it was allowed no tanks or heavy artillery. Manufacturing these in secret was one way of creating work. Similarly, Germans were not allowed to build big naval vessels. So Hitler concentrated on so-called 'pocket battleships' which had an astonishing speed and fire-power for their tonnage. No military aeroplanes were allowed, but German pilots had for a long time been training in gliders and airliners. A new aircraft-manufacturing industry was one more means of making work where none had been before.

Though Germans were not as well off as some other European nations – 'guns before butter' was the motto of Reichsmarshal Hermann Goering – they were by no means starving, as they had been in the early 1920s, or facing a future of unemployment as they had been after 1929. All this helped to quell people's doubts.

Jewish men and women forced to scrub the streets of Vienna in November 1938. People crowd to watch, and Hitler Youth stand over them.

Hitler brings back respect

A further reason for Hitler's popularity was the way he restored national pride to Germany. He had always promised to remove the humiliations imposed by the Treaty of Versailles, and the rearmament programme was essential for that. In March 1935 he introduced military conscription. He also ordered a period of work in the Labour Service which every fit young man had to undergo, digging ditches, building foundations for roads, and preparing bridges. These measures meant that a large army could quickly be formed. In March 1936, amid general rejoicing, he marched his troops across the Rhine bridges and established his right to occupy the whole of the Rhineland. That same year he entered on an agreement with the Italian dictator Mussolini, establishing the Berlin–Rome 'axis' or alliance.

So far, he had not gone outside German frontiers. Earlier, however, he had attempted to join Austria with Germany, for which purpose the Austrian Chancellor Dollfuss had been murdered on 24 July 1934 by Austrian Nazis. (Hitler's conni-

A cartoon by Low which appeared in the London 'Evening Standard', 18 February 1938.

" Why should we take a stand about someone pushing someone else when it's all so far away.. "

BRITAIN
FRANCE
N.W.EUROPE
NR.EAST
BALKANS
AUSTRIA
CZECH.
BRITISH EMPIRE

LOW

INCREASING PRESSURE.

Crowds gathered at Nuremberg in 1938 were treated to a demonstration of German military strength as tanks and infantry engaged in mock battle.

German expansion to 1 September 1939

Germany 1933
Remilitarised 1936
Annexed 1938
Annexed 1939
Protectorate established 1939

vance was never proved, but never much doubted.) In March 1938 the vital step was taken. German troops marched into Austria, meeting no resistance, and incorporated the country into what was now known as Greater Germany. Some Austrians welcomed this. As German-speakers, they had hoped to join Germany when the Austro-Hungarian Empire broke up in 1918. Others, especially Jews and Socialists, suddenly found their existence threatened. Yet this *Anschluss*, or joining, could to some extent be justified on one of the principles of Versailles, which stated that all people of one nationality had a right to live under one government. Austrians were not Germans, but sufficiently close to them for a smokescreen defence of the invasion to be created.

No such defence could be made of Hitler's next move, made on the pretext that many Germans living in the border regions of Czechoslovakia, the 'Sudetenland', were being harassed. For a short while he persuaded the British Prime Minister, Neville Chamberlain, that he was justified in seizing an area of 29,000 square kilometres (11,200 square miles). This was at the Munich Conference of 29 September 1938. The invasion and occupation of half of Czechoslovakia in March 1939

could not be justified under any circumstances. It was a clear indication to the rest of the world that Hitler would stop at nothing. In fact the British government was now secretly warned by two men close to Hitler that Poland would be next, in a few months' time.

For Germans not threatened by Nazism, all these gains in territory were a source of pride and enthusiasm. They did not expect a war. Hitler himself perhaps did not, though he announced that he meant shortly to invade Poland at a meeting of generals on 23 May 1939. Having got so far by bluff, he may have thought that little or no resistance would be offered. There, however, he was wrong.

The leaders of the Third Reich

Martin Bormann

Martin Bormann, born 1900, joined the Nazi Party, 1927. Steadily rose in the party, becoming Chief of Staff to Hess, 1933, member of the Reichstag, 1934. After war broke out, gradually ousted all other rivals and became Hitler's closest associate and adviser, with almost total power in Third Reich. After Hitler's death, disappeared from the Berlin bunker; may have died in Berlin in those last days but rumours persist that he is still alive in South America.

Josef Goebbels

Josef Goebbels, born 1897, educated Bonn and Heidelberg universities, became a journalist. Joined Nazi Party, 1926, became Gauleiter of Berlin-Brandenburg, November 1926, chief of Party propaganda, 1929, Minister of Propaganda and Popular Enlightenment in Third Reich, 1933. As such, operated extremely powerful propaganda machine, totally without moral scruple, in which respect for truth played no part, subordinating all to the glorification of Hitler, his ideas and his régime. Goebbels was bitterly aware of being himself the antithesis of the Nazi idea of manhood: small, dark, with a crippled leg and permanent limp. Remained with Hitler in Berlin bunker as the Russians approached, 1945. After Hitler's death, he and his wife poisoned their six small children and then committed suicide.

Hermann Goering

Hermann Goering, born 1893, served in the air force in First World War, becoming commander of the famous Richthofen air circus. Joined Nazi Party, 1922, took part in the Munich putsch of 1923, then left Germany. Returned and became Nazi member of Reichstag, 1928, Prime Minister of Prussia and Minister of the Interior, 1933, organising political police which was later incorporated into Gestapo. Became head of the air force, 1935, responsible for building up Germany's air power; 1939, chairman of the Cabinet council for the defence of the Reich and designated Hitler's successor. At first very close to Hitler, supported his aggressive policies and took a large part in planning for war. The failure of the Luftwaffe in the Battle of Britain in 1940 and afterwards over Germany led to his decline in power and loss of Hitler's confidence. Condemned to death at Nuremberg trials, managed to commit suicide in his cell, 1946.

Rudolf Hess

Rudolf Hess, born 1894, the son of a German merchant, served in air force in First World War. Joined Nazi Party, 1920, becoming close friend of Hitler, was with him at the Munich putsch in 1923 and

confined with him at Landsberg; worked with him there on *Mein Kampf.* Became Hitler's private secretary, 1923, chairman of the Central Political Bureau of the Nazi Party, 1932 and deputy Führer, 1933. Always totally loyal to Hitler, there was astonishment and disbelief when he flew alone to Scotland in 1941, parachuted down and asked to talk to the Duke of Hamilton. Probably aimed to negotiate a compromise between Britain and Germany but these attempts ignored and his sanity questioned. Tried at Nuremberg and sentenced to life imprisonment in Spandau prison. He was still there in 1981.

Heinrich Himmler

Heinrich Himmler, born 1900, joined Nazi Party 1923, took part in Munich putsch, 1923, became head of the SS, 1929 and of Gestapo, 1936. As such had enormous power in Germany, as head of vast machine for political oppression and terror. 1939, became responsible for 'purifying' the German nation; established network of concentration camps, devised methods of mass murder and medical 'experiment' and planned extermination of Jews, Poles, Russians, gypsies. In command of the final defence of Berlin, 1945, escaped after German surrender, was recaptured but managed to commit suicide.

Wilhelm Keitel

Wilhelm Keitel, born 1882, a career soldier, served in the First World War, became Hitler's chief of the armed forces high command, 1938. Remained at that post throughout the war, totally subservient to Hitler in whom he believed absolutely. Tried at Nuremberg, and hanged, 1946.

Albert Speer

Albert Speer, born 1905, became an architect. He joined the Nazi Party 1931. Soon came to Hitler's attention and was set to work to provide the architectural background to the Third Reich with grandiose plans for monuments, palaces, triumphal arches. Became Minister of Armaments and Munitions, 1942, and made continuation of the war possible by gigantic increase of armament production. Tried at Nuremberg and sentenced to twenty years in Spandau Prison, the only defendant to admit his own guilt. Release, 1966.

Julius Streicher

Julius Streicher, born 1895, became a school-teacher. After serving in First World War, began violently anti-Jewish, nationalistic political movement in Nuremberg. Joined the Nazi Party 1929, became Gauleiter at Nuremberg and Nazi member of the Reichstag, 1933. Became a major propagandist of Nazi party, publishing *Der Stürmer*, a weekly newspaper totally devoted to vicious, frequently obscene attacks on the Jews. A brutal sadist, his behaviour alarmed even the Nazi hierarchy and led to his removal from Party posts in 1940, although his propaganda continued. Tried at Nuremberg and hanged, 1946.

5 The new order in Europe

A Polish farmer, still at work in the fields as German tanks rumble past, September 1939.

Conquest without peace

The attack on Poland which began on 1 September 1939 was a *Blitzkrieg*, a lightning war, in which German forces, spearheaded by tanks and bombers, crushed all organised resistance in just over two weeks. Having signed a treaty of non-aggression with Stalin, Hitler could reckon on keeping the Soviet Union quiet for some time to come. He had now regained the Polish 'corridor,' restored Danzig as a German city, and had a springboard prepared for an invasion of Russia. Only in Russia and its bordering states, as he had said in *Mein Kampf*, could Germany gain the territory it needed to hold its expanding population. The treaty with Stalin was not meant to last; Hitler had intended to invade Russia since 1924.

The rapid conquest of Poland did not lead to peace. Both Britain and France declared war on Germany and although neither country was prepared, Hitler became aware that he now had to re-cast his plans. For nearly a year, the German army sat in its string of fortresses along the western frontier, the 'Siegfried Line,' while the French sat in their 'Maginot Line' and only a few skirmishes took place. Then in April 1940, Hitler occupied Denmark and Norway. A month later, instead of attacking the Maginot Line, he by-passed it, invading the Netherlands, Belgium and Luxemburg, and sending his tanks speeding down the roads behind the French armies towards the Mediterranean, cutting off supplies and reserves. The British army was forced to one side and retreated to the coast. It only escaped by bringing every available boat to rescue the troops from the harbour and beaches of Dunkirk. Six weeks after the attack had begun, France surrendered.

But the Channel stopped further advance, and with the defeat of the *Luftwaffe* (the German air force) by Britain's Royal Air Force, Hitler turned his attentions first to the Balkans, then to Russia. In June 1941 he attacked so suc-

Poles rounded up and searched in 1939. Such a scene could have been witnessed daily in most parts of Europe for the next five and a half years.

cessfully that in ten weeks the German armies were outside Leningrad. After that, progress was much slower. Late in 1942 the tide began to turn against Germany. The British victory at El Alamein in North Africa was followed in November by a Russian counter-attack which eventually forced into surrender a huge German army freezing in the cold in Stalingrad. Then began a retreat in which the Germans fought every inch of the way.

They now had to spread their numbers across Europe from the Black Sea to the Pyrenees and from the Alps to the Arctic Circle. Every country they had occupied organised secret groups of resisters who blew up trains, supplied intelligence to the Allied forces, ambushed small companies of troops, and helped Allied prisoners of war and pilots who had crashed to escape to neutral countries. Although there had been at first quite a large number of pro-German sympathisers in the occupied countries, the Germans were now hated on all sides. Torture and harsh imprisonment by the Gestapo and the SS aroused resistance and could not break the will to fight back.

The struggle against Communism

Hitler had Japan and Italy as allies, but the war against the USSR, the only war of importance to him so long as the British and Americans did not open a 'second front' by attacking him in Europe, was entirely his own concern. In an attempt at

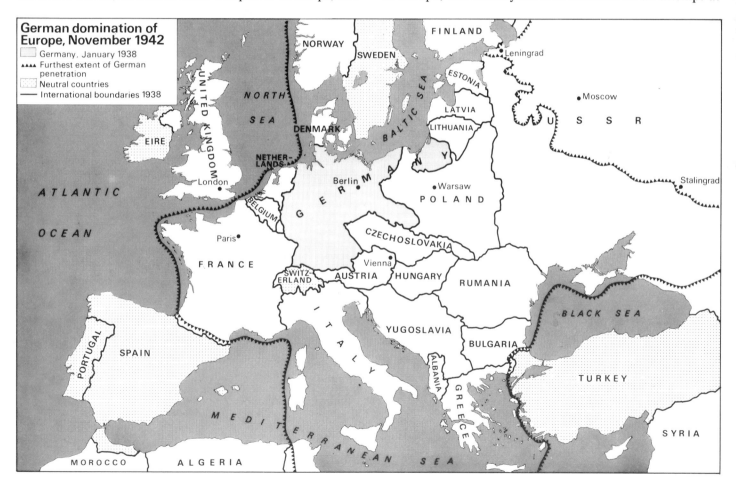

German domination of Europe, November 1942

- Germany, January 1938
- ▲▲▲ Furthest extent of German penetration
- Neutral countries
- International boundaries 1938

winning over the peoples of Europe, he represented his war as a crusade against Bolshevism. This had been enough of a threat in earlier years to gain the Pope's acquiescence as well as that of Britain and France. Now it gained him a little support from some French, Poles (the Poles having a long-standing tradition of enmity towards Russia) and members of other nations who joined the legions of foreigners fighting on his side. There were even some 200,000 Soviet refugees or former prisoners in these legions, for the methods of the Communists under Stalin had been not much different from those of the Nazis themselves.

What Hitler had in mind was not a free union of European nations, but a 'Greater German Reich.' In this state, the Scandinavians and Dutch, whom he regarded, much to their resentment, as practically Germans, would have a share, but the Slavs would be decimated, sent to Siberia, or used as slaves. The French and Italians, though not Slavs, were not Nordic either. Recruits from these and other European countries were therefore not easily found, and the terrorist tactics of the SS deterred some who might have otherwise volunteered. It is true that many co-operated nevertheless: about a million non-Germans fought or worked in the German forces. But Hitler was increasingly forced to rely for fighting soldiers on Germans only, an unwelcome prospect as losses on the Russian front reached high figures. Old men and young teenagers had to be drafted.

Europe under the terror

The record of German military action in these years was sometimes unusually barbaric. The German air force began the heavy bombing of open towns. Russian prisoners of war were treated with a harshness contrary to the Geneva Convention safeguarding their welfare: it is maintained that 3 million Russian prisoners were killed by the army, co-operating with the SS. Innocent civilians in occupied countries were shot in large numbers, in reprisal for attacks on the army made by other civilians. But it was not the regular army which burned the entire population of a French village in the church of Oradour-sur-Glane, or eradicated the village of Lidice in Czechoslovakia; it was the *Waffen-SS*, the notorious military wing of the SS, which by 1943 numbered 450,000 volunteers. Nor was it the German armed services that devised ingenious

tortures to wrest secrets from the members of resistance movements: it was the Gestapo. Similarly, it was the SS and the Gestapo who sent trainloads of men and women from occupied countries to forced labour in German factories and mines, freeing Germans for military service.

At the same time, there were some policies which involved all the fighting services and for which there was no rational explanation, except perhaps that Nazi leaders now had virtually insane ideas about the need for maintaining a healthy

France 1942. Victor Fajnzylber, a war invalid, wearing medals for bravery. His six-year-old daughter wears a yellow Star of David, as every Jew of six years or more had to do throughout occupied Europe, and in Germany itself after September 1941. This man was exempt from wearing the star because he was a French national hero, but was later deported to an extermination camp.

Anne Frank, born 1929 of German Jewish parents who emigrated to the Netherlands. After the German invasion of 1940, she and her family lived in a secret apartment in a house in Amsterdam. There she wrote the famous diary which was later published. She died in March 1945 in the concentration camp of Bergen-Belsen.

above: *Dutch Jews being transported to the extermination camp at Auschwitz.*

below: *Hungarian Jews wait in a thicket near the Auschwitz gas-chambers. The women and children with the elderly and sick were usually the first to be killed. This photograph taken in 1944 is the last record of any of these people.*

race. Between 1938 and 1941, in certain hospitals, over 70,000 mentally infirm and 'unproductive' citizens were put to death. Although this massacre ceased because of protests made by Bishop von Galen (who had only a few years earlier prayed for God's blessing on Hitler), it was the prelude to a much more widespread attempt at racial purity.

The reason for the extermination of Jews which now began is sometimes given as the fear of military defeat before the 'Jewish problem' had been solved. But Hitler had proposed the killing of all Jews in Europe in January 1939, and as early as 1940 the Jews of Poland were being forcibly driven from their homes and sent to work camps; $2\frac{1}{2}$ million of them died as a result. German Jews were forbidden to use public transport, or to buy books or newspapers; their ration cards were made invalid. By May 1941, orders were being given to shoot all male Jews, Communist officials, 'inferior Asiatics' and gypsies in occupied Eastern Europe. One special unit alone reported 229,052 executions by shooting or gassing by the beginning of 1942. All these killings were inspired by theories about the purity or superiority of the German race.

The *systematic* killing of all Jews was being planned in May 1941, and began in June 1942, though for a time it was pretended that the trainloads of people being sent to extermination camps were 'being emigrated', as the odd phrase went. They were persuaded to enter large gas-chambers said to be for disinfection, though in fact the thousands of naked men, women and children who did enter them were gassed, and their bodies either burned or buried in mass-graves; their hair, gold teeth, and anything else that could be used were taken

Jewish women at Auschwitz being herded to work, 1944. Note their shaved heads and coarse clothes.

German concentration camps

Neuengamme
Bergen-Belsen
Ravensbrück
Hanover
Oranienburg (Sachsenhausen)
Berlin
Vught
Dora-Mittelbau
Buchenwald
Weimar
Gross-Rosen
GERMAN REICH
Theresienstadt
Prague
Flossenbürg
Natzweiler
Dachau
Munich
Vienna
Mauthausen

TREBLINKA
Warsaw
CHELMNO
Lodz
SOBIBOR
Lublin
MAJDANEK
AUSCHWITZ
BELZEC
Krakow
Lvov

0   200 km
0   100 miles

☐ German Reich 31 Dec 1939
— National frontiers Jan 1938
+ Extermination camps
☆ Main concentration camps (there were 22 in all, and 165 labour camps)

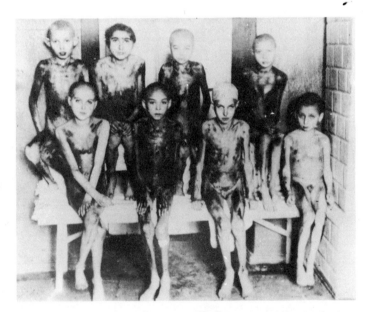

These children survived Auschwitz; this is how they looked when they were freed. If liberation had not come they would probably have been killed, used for experiments or have starved to death.

first from their corpses. At least 4 million Jews were killed in this way, and another 2 million by other methods. Some who were not killed were subjected to painful medical experiments which crippled them permanently.

Though the extermination camps were run by the SS, in many places the armed forces worked in close co-operation. Distinguishing between Nazis and ordinary Germans is not easy in this case, though some people were entirely ignorant of the whole matter. All the extermination camps were in Poland, where ordinary Germans were not able to witness what went on.

Why did the Germans support the war?

The early excitement and pride in victory did not wear off in 1939 as it had done in 1914. The attack on Russia in 1941 was hailed with enthusiasm as long as it was brilliantly successful. When the pace of advance slowed down, and freezing cold made life almost impossible, soldiers feared surrendering to the Russians, who were reputed to shoot their prisoners. They also feared that a Communist régime would be established by the Russians in Germany, and so they tried fanatically to avoid defeat. Discipline was rigid, and disobedience could be punished by transfer to one of the 'penal battalions', which were given particularly dangerous jobs.

An ingrained habit of obedience also prevented protest. At Auschwitz extermination camp the officials would sometimes ask why they must go on with the massacres for month after month. The commandant replied that, though he felt pity, he could not let himself show emotion. 'I had to do all this, because I was the one everybody looked up to, because I had to show that I not only gave orders, made arrangements, but was prepared to be present everywhere, just as I demanded from those under my command.' Himmler, head of the SS, also told his generals that they must deliberately suppress any personal feelings they had for a particular Jew. Racial theory mattered more than liking someone.

There were, however, soldiers and civilians who opposed Hitler from the moment the war started. One general tried to arrest him soon after 3 September 1939. Several officers attempted to assassinate him between 1939 and 1943, but all failed. Many exiled German writers, including Thomas Mann, denounced him from abroad. Communists were organised in a group known as 'The Red Orchestra'. The 'Confessing Church' opposed the official state Church, and protested at some of the worst injustices. A small group of students who called themselves 'The White Rose' distributed leaflets in 1943 and chalked 'Down with Hitler' on the walls of Munich; they were arrested and beheaded. Finally, Colonel von Stauffenberg, Chief of Staff to the Commander-in-Chief of the Home Army, decided to use his privilege of sitting near Hitler in his secret hide-out, 'The Wolf's Lair'. On 20 July 1944 he walked into the room where Hitler was to meet Mussolini, left a briefcase with a time-bomb in it, and walked out. But the briefcase was by chance moved behind the leg of a table, and exploded fairly harmlessly. All the field-marshals and generals and other conspirators who had supported von Stauffenberg either killed themselves or were arrested and gruesomely hanged.

From then till the end of the war nearly a year later, every regiment and ship had a Nazi commissar appointed to see that the Party rather than the High Command always had the last word. The Germans fought on with even greater tenacity, knowing that disobedience could mean execution, but never showing any sign of mutiny. It is sometimes said that the Allied policy of 'unconditional surrender' inspired them to fight more strongly; not knowing what might follow defeat, they struggled on. But the way they fought till the very last minute when all possible hope had gone suggests another equally possible explanation. There was a widespread mystical belief that total defeat was the necessary prelude to a real rebirth, and some German soldiers at any rate were inspired by such perverse notions.

The destruction of Germany

Stauffenberg's attempt on 20 July 1944 was made when the end seemed near. On 6 June the Allied forces in the west had landed in Normandy in the north of France, opening a second front, and by 20 July had begun to burst through the German defences. On 15 August there were landings in the south of France, and on 6 October the Russians entered Hungary. The Allies had landed in Italy in September 1943, forcing the Germans into a slow retreat. 'Thousand-bomber raids' from bases in Britain were destroying German cities area by area.

Still the Germans resisted. German troops massacred a great part of the population of Warsaw during an uprising. Flying-bomb and rocket-bomb attacks on London began. Hitler had hopes of making an atom bomb before the Americans did: had he succeeded, the victory might even then have been his. (It is said that German atomic scientists deliberately slowed down research to frustrate him.) Even as late as December 1944, a counter-offensive through the Ardennes in Belgium looked dangerously like succeeding.

The Allied pincers went on closing. On 7 March 1945 the Americans crossed the Rhine. On 21 April the Russians reached Berlin, where Hitler was now hiding in a bomb-proof shelter, the 'Bunker', pretending to control operations. On 26 April Russian and American troops actually met in the middle of Germany, yet the German armed forces did not surrender till 7 May.

Hitler committed suicide on 30 April, together with his mistress Eva Braun, whom he had married at the last moment. Goebbels and Himmler also took their own lives. Berlin and almost every other German city and town were by now reduced to rubble. It seemed that the Nazi era had ended once and for all.

6 Hitler's legacy

Human rights and human duty

In 1946 those Nazi leaders who had survived were tried by an international court at Nuremberg. The head of the Luftwaffe, Hermann Goering, the Foreign Minister von Ribbentrop, and ten other leaders were sentenced to death. The court found the German government guilty of war crimes 'on a vast scale, never before seen in the history of war, attended by every conceivable circumstance of cruelty and horror'. In all, 12 million non-combatants, including 6 million Jews, had been exterminated, but this figure did not include the 55 million soldiers and civilians of all nations killed in fighting and bombing.

These trials were a new development in international law. It was argued against them that judges and prosecuting counsel were citizens of nations with which Germany had been at war, and must be biased, though it would in practice have been difficult to find others qualified for the task. The truth of the evidence against the Nazis was not in serious doubt.

No court had ever had to deal with killings on such an unheard-of scale. There was nothing relating to them in international law, and the court had to proceed from certain assumptions about human rights. The defence often advanced the argument that soldiers were obliged to obey orders even though they went against the grain. This the court denied: though discipline is necessary, there are limits beyond which no soldier has a right to go. A dilemma remained. Was it right for British and American airmen to obey orders which resulted in the burning down of the city of Dresden at such speed that thousands of civilians were incinerated? Was it right to drop atom bombs on Hiroshima and Nagasaki? Hitler's policies and those of the Japanese perhaps left no alternative. But the twentieth century has still not resolved this matter of conscience.

A Berlin street in August 1946, 15 months after Germany's defeat. The city, badly damaged by bombing and street-warfare, was divided into sectors occupied by the British, the French, the Americans and the Russians.

In 1949, the first three sectors became part of the Federal Republic of Germany (West Germany), while the fourth became the capital of the German Democratic Republic (East Germany).

Germany divided

The year in which the war ended is sometimes called in Germany 'Anno Zero'. The country was divided into zones of occupation under the supervision of British, American, French and Russian troops. This time, however, defeated Germany was not treated as it had been in 1919. The USSR did remove the contents of factories to replace those destroyed in Russia, but the USA supplied western Germany with economic aid under the Marshall Plan. In 1949 the two parts of Germany became separate states, the Federal Republic, a parliamentary democracy, in the West, and the Democratic Republic, a democracy in the Communist sense, in the East. Both sides accused each other of continuing Nazi traditions. Both sides soon rebuilt their ruined cities and established themselves as the most prosperous countries in Western and Eastern Europe respectively. Neither has reverted to the theories and practice of Nazism, though the Democratic Republic imposes strict censorship, imprisons or exiles liberal writers and critics of the régime, and prevents its citizens by a wall and fence guarded by armed sentries from leaving for the West. Hitler's memory enjoys little popularity, though small neo-Nazi (new Nazi) groups exist in the Federal Republic, and both republics have employed in senior positions men who were previously Nazis. Their excuse was that until the next generations grew up, as they have now done, there was no alternative.

What most surprised foreigners in 1945 was that Germans suddenly rejected or ignored almost everything Hitler had stood for. The fanaticism and later tenacity which had lasted twelve years vanished overnight. Only in Eastern Germany do the youth organisations, the para-military training given to factory workers, and the suppression of free thought bear any resemblance to the Nazi era, though there is no such brutality as existed then. In Western Germany, whatever its faults, including perhaps discrimination against Communists (*Berufsverbot*), genuine parliamentary democracy has been established for a longer period than any before in German history.

The legend

There were some Germans who refused to believe, after 1945, that the Nazis had been guilty of the evils of which they were now accused. Some maintained that Germany had been saving Europe from Bolshevism, and should be thanked for it. Many more were glad it was all over, and ashamed, secretly or openly, at their own acquiescence. A few ex-SS members still hold rallies, and ex-soldiers sometimes make out that though they always detested Hitler, they had to do their duty for their country. Fear of an eventual Nazi revival is not wholly unjustified.

Even outside Germany Nazi ideas still have a romantic appeal for people who like the idea of looking demonic. Nazi insignia, badges and daggers have become so popular in Britain and the USA that imitations are now manufactured to meet the demand. Swastikas are painted on the walls in many European countries but they represent a rebellious spirit rather than a programme. Weak neo-Nazi parties exist in Britain, other European countries and the USA.

Though Hitler was defeated, the history of the world since his time has seen an unparalleled increase in dictatorships which rely on torture, mass killings, and suppression of free speech. Modern weapons and policing equipment make their success easier. But parliamentary democracies too are more numerous and stronger than they have ever been. They, rather than the dictatorships, are still the best form of government for civilised peoples. But as the history of the Weimar Republic shows, democracy can be totally destroyed in only a few years.

The Hitler years. Key dates

Weimar Germany

1919   28 June: Peace Treaty signed at Versailles   *p.6*

          12 September: Hitler's first speech at a DAP (later NSDAP) meeting

1921   Collapse of the mark

1923   11 January: French occupy Ruhr (until July 1925)   *p.8*

          8–9 November: Munich putsch   *p.9*

1924   Hitler writes *Mein Kampf* (first volume published 1925)   *p.9*

1926   8 September: Germany admitted to League of Nations   *p.10*

1929   October: Wall Street crash   *p.11*

1930   14 September: Reichstag elections – sudden Nazi rise to being second biggest party   *pp.11–12*

Nazi Germany

1933   30 January: Hitler appointed Chancellor   *p.13*

          27 February: Reichstag fire   *p.14*

          23 March: Enabling Act – Hitler given dictatorial power   *p.14*

          14 October: Germany resigns from League of Nations

1934   30 June: 'Night of the Long Knives'   *p.17*

          19 August: Plebiscite approves Hitler as Führer

1935   13 January: Saar plebiscite (rejoined Germany, 7 March)

          15 September: Nuremberg Laws – Jews deprived of citizenship   *p.17*

1936   7 March: German troops reoccupy Rhineland   *p.20*

          1 August: Opening of Olympic Games in Berlin   *p.19*

          27 October: Formation of Rome–Berlin Axis   *p.20*

          17 November: Japan and Germany make pact against Communism

1938   11 March: German troops enter Austria (Anschluss declared, 13th)   *p.21*

          September: Czechoslovak crisis (Munich agreement, 29th)   *p.21*

1939   15 March: Germany takes Bohemia and Moravia as protectorates   *p.21*

The Second World War

1939   1 September: German invasion of Poland – Blitzkrieg   *p.24*

1940   April: German conquest of Denmark, Norway   *p.24*

          May–June: German conquest of Netherlands, Belgium, Luxemburg, France   *p.24*

1941   April: German conquest of Yugoslavia, Greece   *p.24*

          22 June: 'Barbarossa' – German invasion of USSR   *pp.24–5*

          7 December: Pearl Harbor – Japan and USA enter war

1942   23 October: El Alamein – the turn of the tide in North Africa   *p.25*

1943   31 January: Surrender at Stalingrad – the turn of the tide in Russia   *p.25*

          10 July: Allied landing in Sicily (Italy, 3 September)   *p.29*

1944   6 June: 'D-Day' – Allied landing in Normandy   *p.29*

1945   30 April: Hitler commits suicide   *p.29*

Index

Allies, 25, 29
Alsace-Lorraine, 6
American forces in World War II, 29
Anschluss, 21
anti-Semitism, 12-13, 16-17
'Aryan race', 16
assassination attempts against
   Hitler, 29
atom bomb, 29, 30
Auschwitz, 18, 29
Austria, 4, 20-21

Bauhaus, 10
Berlin-Rome axis, 20
Bismarck (Prussian minister), 4, 16
Blitzkrieg (lightning war), 24
Blockleiter, 18
Bolshevik Revolution, 5, 12
Bolshevism, 6, 26
Bormann, Martin, 22
Braun, Eva, 29
Brest-Litovsk, Treaty of, 6
Britain, 24-25, 26, 29
Brüning (German Chancellor), 11, 13
'Bunker, the', 29

Chamberlain, Neville, 21
Communism, 6, 8, 14; Hitler's
   attitude towards, 9, 26
Communist Party of Germany, 6, 7,
   11, 13
concentration camps, 13, 17-18
'Confessing Church', 29
Czechoslovakia, invasion of, 21

Dachau, 13
Danzig, 6, 24
Dawes Plan, 10

Denmark, invasion of, 24
Dollfus (Austrian Chancellor), 20-21
Dunkirk, 24

Einstein, Albert, 10
El Alamein, 25
'Enabling Act,' 14
extermination camps, 27-28

Fascist Party (Italy), 8
Federal Republic of Germany, 31
France, 4, 24, 25
Freikorps, 6, 8
Furtwängler, Wilhelm, 10

Gauen, 16
Geneva Convention, 26
German army, rearmament of, 19, 20
German Democratic Republic, 30
German Workers' Party, 8, 9
Gestapo, 17, 26
Goebbels, Josef, 18, 22, 29
Goering, Herman, 19, 22, 30
Göttingen, university of, 10
Gropius, Walter, 10

Hegel (philosopher), 15
Hess, Rudolf, 22-23
Himmler, Heinrich, 17, 23, 29
Hindemith, Paul, 10
Hindenburg, Field-Marshal and
   President, 10, 13, 14
Hitler Jugend (Hitler Youth), 12, 14, 18
Hugenberg, Alfred, 12

Italy, 8, 20, 25

Japan, 25

Jews, 16, 17; extermination of, 27, 30; German attitudes towards, 8, 9, 10, 12-13

Kandinsky, Wassily, 10
Keitel, Wilhelm, 23
Klee, Paul, 10
Kokoschaka, Oscar, 10

League of Nations, 10
Lenin, 5
Leningrad, 25
Lidice, 26
Liebknecht, Karl, 6
Locarno Agreements, 10
Ludendorff, Field-Marshal, 4, 9
Luftwaffe, 24, 26, 30
Luxemburg, Rosa, 6

Maginot Line, 24
Mann, Thomas, 29
Marne, battle of, 4
Marshall Plan, 31
'master race', doctrine of, 9
Mein Kampf, 9, 24
militarism in Germany, 6
Mosley, Sir Oswald, 8
Mussolini, 8, 20

National Socialist Party, 8, 11-12, 14, 15; founding of, 7; programme of, 12, 13
Nazi party. *See* National Socialist Party
Nietzsche, Friedrich, 6, 10, 16-17
'Night of the Long Knives', 17
Nordic races, 16, 26
Normandy landing, 29
Norway, invasion of, 24

Nuremberg, 12, 18; Laws, 17; trials, 22-23, 30

Oranienburg, 13

Papen, von (German Chancellor), 13
Pius XI, Pope, 18
Planck, Max, 10
Poland, invasion of, 21, 24
Polish 'corridor', 6, 24
Protocols of the Elders of Zion, 16
Prussia, 6, 13, 14
putsch, Munich, 9

'Red Orchestra, The', 29
Reichstag, 12, 13, 14
reparations, German, after World War I, 6, 8, 9-10
resistance movements, 25
Ribbentrop, von (German Foreign Minister), 30
Rome, comparison of, to Nazi state, 15
Royal Air Force (British), 24
Ruhr, French occupation of, 8
Russia, 4, 8, 16, 26, 28-29, 31; Bolshevik Revolution in, 4, 5; German invasion of, 24-25; treaty of, with Germany, 24
Russian Revolution, 4, 5

Schleicher, von (German Chancellor), 13
Schutzstaffeln (SS), 14, 17-18, 26, 28
Siegfried Line, 24
Social Democrat Party (German), 4-6, 7, 12, 13
Socialists, 4, 8
Spartacists, 6

Speer, Albert, 23
SS *(Schutzstaffeln),* 14, 17-18, 26, 28
Stalin, 8, 13, 24
Stalingrad, 25
Stauffenberg, von, 29
Stein, Edith, 18
Stormtroopers, 12, 13, 14, 15, 17
Streicher, Julius, 23
Stresemann (German Foreign Minister), 10
Sturm-Abteilung (SA), 12
Sudentenland, 21

Thyssen, Fritz, 12
Triumph of the Will, The, 18

Union of Fascists, British, 8

Vatican, relation of, with Nazis, 14, 26
Versailles, Treaty of, 6, 9, 12, 19, 20, 21

Waffen-SS, 26
Wagner, Richard, 16
Walter, Bruno, 10
Weill, Kurt, 10
Weimar Constitution, 7, 10, 14
'White Rose, The', 29
Wiechert, Ernst, 17
Wilhelm II, 4

Zentrum party, 7, 12, 13

Acknowledgments

The author and publisher would like to thank the following for permission to reproduce illustrations:
front cover, pp. 1, 7, 15, 17, 19, 21, 24, 30 BBC Hulton Picture Library; back cover, p. 20 (below) London Express News and Feature Services; pp. 8, 12 Langewiesche-Brandt (from Friedrich Arnold, *Anschläge, Deutsche Plakate als Dokumente der Zeit 1900–1960*, 1963); p. 9 Ullstein Bilderdienst; p. 10 Various Designers, Bauhaus Design Items from the Collections of the Museum of Modern Art, New York; pp. 11, 16 Gertrud Heartfield; p. 14 Institute of Contemporary History and Wiener Library; p. 18 Interfoto Pressebild Agentur; pp. 20 (above), 27, 28 Yad Vashem Archives; p. 26 Centre de Documentation Juive Contemporaine, Paris.

Maps by Reg Piggott
Portrait drawings by Ian Newsham

front cover: *Adolf Hitler (1889–1945) photographed in the 1920s in Brownshirt uniform.*

back cover: *By the mid 1930s, some people in Britain were aware of the danger of what Hitler was doing in Germany and where this could lead. Drawing by the famous cartoonist David Low for the London 'Evening Standard', 8 July 1936.*

title page: *Parade of Nazi party banners with the swastika emblem carried by members of the SA (Sturm-Abteilung) at Nuremberg in 1933, the year Hitler came to power.*

The Cambridge History Library

The Cambridge Introduction to History
Written by Trevor Cairns

PEOPLE BECOME CIVILIZED	EUROPE AND THE WORLD
THE ROMANS AND THEIR EMPIRE	THE BIRTH OF MODERN EUROPE
BARBARIANS, CHRISTIANS, AND MUSLIMS	THE OLD REGIME AND THE REVOLUTION
THE MIDDLE AGES	POWER FOR THE PEOPLE
EUROPE AROUND THE WORLD	

The Cambridge Topic Books
General Editor Trevor Cairns

THE AMERICAN WAR OF INDEPENDENCE	LIFE IN A MEDIEVAL VILLAGE
BENIN: AN AFRICAN KINGDOM AND CULTURE	LIFE IN THE IRON AGE
THE BUDDHA	LIFE IN THE OLD STONE AGE
BUILDING THE MEDIEVAL CATHEDRALS	THE MAORIS
CHINA AND MAO ZEDONG	MARTIN LUTHER
CHRISTOPHER WREN AND ST. PAUL'S CATHEDRAL	MEIJI JAPAN
	THE MURDER OF ARCHBISHOP THOMAS
THE EARLIEST FARMERS AND THE FIRST CITIES	MUSLIM SPAIN
EARLY CHINA AND THE WALL	THE NAVY THAT BEAT NAPOLEON
THE FIRST SHIPS AROUND THE WORLD	THE PARTHENON
GANDHI AND THE STRUGGLE FOR INDIA'S INDEPENDENCE	POMPEII
	THE PYRAMIDS
HERNAN CORTES: CONQUISTADOR IN MEXICO	THE ROMAN ARMY
HITLER AND THE GERMANS	THE ROMAN ENGINEERS
THE INDUSTRIAL REVOLUTION BEGINS	ST. PATRICK AND IRISH CHRISTIANITY
LIFE IN A FIFTEENTH-CENTURY MONASTERY	THE VIKING SHIPS

The Cambridge History Library will be expanded in the future to include additional volumes. Lerner Publications Company is pleased to participate in making this excellent series of books available to a wide audience of readers.

Lerner Publications Company
241 First Avenue North, Minneapolis, Minnesota 55401